# Higher Heights, Deeper Depths In Christ

(HOW TO REACH YOUR DESTINY WITH GOD)

## Candace L. Strand

WESTBOW
PRESS®
A DIVISION OF THOMAS NELSON
& ZONDERVAN

WestBow Press books may be ordered through booksellers or by contacting:

WestBow Press
A Division of Thomas Nelson & Zondervan
1663 Liberty Drive
Bloomington, IN 47403
www.westbowpress.com
844-714-3454

ISBN: 978-1-6642-4385-9 (sc)
ISBN: 978-1-6642-4386-6 (e)

Library of Congress Control Number: 2021918020

Print information available on the last page.

WestBow Press rev. date: 09/02/2021

# CONTENTS

## APPRECIATION

In writing this book, I give honor to God, my Lord and Savior Jesus Christ, that saved my soul and made me whole. Without God I would be nothing. I am thankful for my family. I appreciate my family. Harry, Charmayne, Angela, I love you. Live holy Cierra, Breonne, Cameron, Kanye, Laila and Kinsley. Carry on with Jesus. Joyce, Mike, Dell, Craig and Doug keep the faith with your families too. Uncle Buddy continue to strive for heaven. I appreciate and miss Mom, Dad, Aunt Thelma, Uncle Paul, Aunt Helen and Aunt Claudette. I also appreciate the many members of the different church families that I was affiliated with throughout the years. Your lives have helped me to become a believer and prayer warrior. I am blessed. God's grace on all. I love you all (Matt. 6:33 KJV).

I am grateful for the mind to be able to write this book. I appreciate my Christian values and morals. As I go through life's journeys being humble and walking in the way of Jesus it helps the light of Christ shine even the more in me.

## FOREWORD

I forward this book to the people of the 21st century generation and beyond who need to be ready for the rapture, to the church, believers of Jesus Christ and Him crucified and resurrection and to the world, of unbelievers of Jesus Christ and Him crucified and resurrected. People should study in order to renew your mind (II. Tim 2:15 KJV), because spiritually you need Christ in order to reach your destiny. Know that, victory is yours, if you only believe. Know that, all things are possible. Time is winding up. Ask yourself, will you be ready when the Lord comes for You? Remember to stay in the scriptures. Continue to reach higher and deeper in Christ.

To my teachers, K-12, my professors at Rowan University (formerly Glassboro State College), ABI Business Institute, Center for Urban Theological Studies (CUTS), Lutheran Theological Seminary at Philadelphia (LTSP) and Newburgh Theological Seminary and College of the Bible, I appreciate my educational training and studies. Thank you!

## INTRODUCTION

In writing this book, I intend to reflect on the steps towards reaching higher heights and deeper depths in the Lord. The Bible tells us how to live holy and how to live right. We must endure as soldiers for the Lord. In order to reach higher heights and deeper depths in Christ you must take a look at the steps listed in this book. They will help you live holy and live right in the world today.

I was led of the Lord to write this book. As ai climbed up Jacob's ladder, I was striving to reach my destiny. As a saved Christian woman, I would like to relate to my experience of moving towards my destiny.

I am old school in a new generation movement. I had to tarry and seek God's face (during the 80's). I had to pray without ceasing along with fasting. Attending church was necessary and enjoyable. I am in my 60's now.

I encourage you to read this book and discover what I had to do to go forth to find out what destiny is. Perhaps your destiny walk maybe different, but I suggest that you let my experience touch your soul.

# PART
# ONE

# RESPECTING OUR SAVIOR

Respect for our Redeemer.
Earnest love of our Maker.
Sincere faith in God.
Practical living and worship, here and abroad.
Effective preaching about the wonderful counselor.
Creative joy in the Lord.
Teaching truth about the Divine one.
By Candace Strand

# CHAPTER 1

# SALVATION (WHAT A MIGHTY GOD WE SERVE)

Salvation is a free gift from God. It is for the sinner.

For wages of sin is death; but the gift of God is eternal life through Jesus Christ our Lord (Romans 6:23 KJV). God will supply all needs for true Christians.

Acts 4:12 (KJV) says, "Neither is there Salvation in any other; for there is none other name under heaven given among men, "whereby we must be saved."

What is the name? The name is Jesus Christ.

You must first repent (Acts 2:38 KJV). People must accept Jesus Christ as their Lord and Savior. For all have sinned, and come short of the glory of God (Romans 3:23 KJV). Ephesians 2:8–9

(KJV) says, For by grace are ye saved through faith; and that not of yourselves; is the gift of God; Not of works, lest any man should boast.

Salvation is received through faith. You must be saved. Salvation is real. It is the state of being saved from sin through Jesus Christ. Romans 10:9 (KJV) says, That if thou shalt confess with thy mouth the Lord Jesus, and shalt believe in thine heart that God hath raised him from the dead, thou shalt be saved. You must be baptized with the Holy Ghost. You must be born again (John 3:7 KJV). The spirit of God is inside the human body. You have keeping power inside and outside you. It brings about a spiritual and natural change in your life. Romans 8:9 (KJV) says, But ye are not in the flesh, but in the Spirit, if so be that the Spirit of God dwell in you. Now if any man have not the Spirit of Christ he is none of His. The Lord will make people glad when people serve Jesus Christ.

The manifestation of the Holy Ghost begins to come forth. The light shines in your life daily. The fruit of the Spirit begins to blossom. Shekinah glory is functional and alive. You're not dead in the spirit anymore. You're alive! Jesus Christ is alive in you. The witness of Jesus Christ is in control. John 1:1, 14 (KJV) says, In the beginning was the Word and the Word was with God, and the Word was God. And the Word was made flesh and dwelt among us, (and we beheld his glory as the only begotten of the father), full of grace and truth. God's Word was in the beginning. Jesus is God. The Bible is about God/Jesus. Jesus came to the world to give up His life for our sin-sick souls. He shed His blood to redeem us. He performed miracles.

He healed the sick, taught, and was that perfect example of love and humility. He did not lie. Jesus never fails. He died on the cross for us. The message of the cross is salvation.

You'll be a witness for Jesus Christ. Salvation stirs you up. You become a servant for Christ. The Great Commission is released in your life (Matthew 19:28–29 KJV). Justice will be done correctly.

Know that eternal life is promised to you. Faith and sanctification are important in salvation also. As you follow sanctification, you are set aside for the service of God. You become consecrated, holy, and pure. Your faith is the substance of things hoped for and the evidence of things not seen. You have a confident belief. You trust God. You have a secure belief in God. There is acceptance of God's will. What a mighty God we serve. Angels bow before him. Heaven and Earth adore him; "What a mighty God we serve."

Romans 8:14–16 (KJV) says that we must sometimes be delivered from some things. Deliverance consists of casting out demons in the Lord Jesus Christ's name. We may have to have all ancestral curses broken and break all soul ties. This procedure also includes pleading the blood of Jesus Christ and asking God to release angels of our Lord for protection. We must bind up principalities, powers, witchcraft, death, and curses. We must continue to call for the warring angels from God to do warfare against demonic forces. The Lord will guide Christians toward the right things.

We must forgive everyone. We must believe that deliverance is what we need. We must not talk to the devil and allow Satan to have control in our lives. We must ask the Lord to fill us with the Holy Ghost and anoint us. We must worship and praise God always. We must have faith. The grace of God is real. Christians must remember the message of the cross. Know that salvation is for everyone. Man, woman, boy, and girl are invited by God to receive the precious gift of salvation and the Holy Ghost. People have to want Jesus Christ in their lives (Acts 2:47 KJV). Christians will be a part of Jesus Christ.

Jesus Christ came to live and die for all of us. That was the purpose of Jesus Christ sacrificing his life. Jesus came to condemn sin and to save us. Jesus Christ wants people to obey the Word of God. When people do that, God will have mercy on people. You are a Christian. God will bless Christians.

# CHAPTER 2

# MILK IS GOOD; IT NOURISHES US

First Peter 2:2–3 (KJV) says, As newborn babes, desire the sincere milk of the word, that ye may grow thereby: If so ye have tasted that the Lord is gracious (Dake 266).

In the natural, a newborn baby loves the milk that is given to him or her. The baby cries. We give the child milk that feeds him or her. The baby receives nourishment that strengthens the body.

The body of Christ has to be a part of growth for new born-again believers. We must encourage, teach, hold up, reprove, rebuke, love, guide, and direct them. The new creature in Christ will grow to be strong and be able to endure hardness. The milk will be a supplement as you go through challenging obstacles and battles.

What is milk?

Milk in the natural is the white fluid with which animals and people feed their young. It is a nutritive substance and simple food. Milk comes from cows, camels (Gen. 32:15 KJV), sheep (Deut. 32:14 KJV), goats (Prov. 27:27 KJV), and a lactating woman.

Milk in the spirit is an inspired and highly prized nourishment. This includes the Word of God, study and reading time, prayer, and Christian music, which involves praise and worship time.

Do not become unskillful. Prepare yourself for daily growth. Hebrews 5:13 (KJV) says, For everyone that useth milk is unskillful in the word of righteousness: for he is a babe (Dake 246). Hebrews 5:14 KJV says, But strong meat belongeth to them that are of full age, even to those who by reason of use have their senses exercised to discern both good and evil (Dake 246).

A bit of history tells us that the Israelites drank sheep and goat milk in the spring and summer. Too much milk is not good for the bones. Sometimes too much milk can cause digestive issues. The Lord wants his people to begin to prepare their digestive systems for meat as we grow in him.

Do not let yourself get weak. Prepare yourself to be able to digest heavier food.

First Corinthians 3:2 (KJV) says, I have fed you with milk, and not with meat: for hitherto ye were not able to bear it, neither yet now are ye able (Dake 177).

Do not become carnal. Stay strong even if you are on milk. Keep yourself encouraged. Know that:

(As you are drinking milk) and as a new creature in Christ you must:

Taste, Sip then …

Drink the milk and continue to grow up daily.

Don't let the milk weigh you down.

Taste and see that the Lord is good. Be reminded that there is more to eating this meal than milk. Your appetite will increase. You will begin to eat vegetables, fruit, meat, and dessert.

Seek the Lord with your whole heart, soul, and mind.

Matthew 7:7 (KJV) says to ask, and it shall be given you; seek and ye shall find; knock and it shall be opened unto you (Dake 6). Enjoy God's nourishment. You will soon be trained on fasting.

Matthew 6:17–18 (KJV) says, but thou, when thou fastest anoint thine head, and wash thy face; That thou appear not unto men to fast, but unto thy Father which is in secret: and thy Father, which seeth in secret, shall reward thee openly (Dake 6).

Matthew 6:33 (KJV) says, But seek ye first the kingdom of God, and his righteousness; and all these things shall be added unto you (Dake 6).

Then the knowledge and understanding will come. Knowledge is the state or fact of knowing, or familiarity, awareness, or understanding gained through experience or study. Learning is the sum or range of what has been perceived or discovered. Knowledge of God closely relates to faith, expressing the perception and understanding of faith (Butler 852). Understanding is the quality of discernment and comprehension; the faculty by which one understands; intelligence, compassionate. A reconciliation of differences. (Berube 886).

With milk, our stomachs are getting ready for meat, fruit, and vegetables. You're going to put on some weight. Sometimes milk coats your stomach. With milk, you will learn how to eat the meat and throw away the bones.

# CHAPTER 3

# HUNGER AND THIRST AFTER RIGHTEOUSNESS

As we hunger and thirst we find that "blessed are they which do hunger and thirst after righteousness: for they shall be filled" (Matt. 5:6 KJV; Scofield 5).

I remember reading the Bible all the time when I was seeking the Holy Ghost. Fasting was also important. Praying and calling on the Lord were natural things to do each day. As I did these daily, the Lord filled me with the Holy Ghost. I believed and trusted God.

What is trust? Well, it's God and faith. It's confidence in the truth of anything; the care of; to believe. Righteousness by hungering and thirsting after God is great. Do it the right way spiritually. I trusted the Lord. I wanted to know the truth about Jesus and the power, and feel the presence of God. I wanted to know the truth about the Word of God.

John 14:6 (Message/Remix)

Jesus said, I am the Road, also the Truth. also the Life. No one gets the father apart from me.

(Peterson, 1,581, 1582)

I wanted to know the truth. Truth is that which is true of according to the facts of the case, agreement with reality and practice of saying or telling. The truth was that I was finally being transformed. My mind was being transformed. I was renewed.

Transform means to change in condition, nature or character; convert. To change in form, appearance or structure, (Berube, 865).

As I was transformed I became a new creature in Christ. The old man was down and the new man was growing in Christ. I looked different, I acted differently and I became more like Jesus. I was made meek and humble and began to live Holy and right. I was baptized in Jesus Christ name and was born again.

Thank you Jesus. Hallelujah!

Acts 1:8 (Message/ Remix) says that, and when the Holy Spirit comes on you, you will be able to be my witnesses in Jerusalem, all over Judea and Samaria, even to the ends of the world. (Peterson, 581).

I was washed by the blood of the lamb. I was overcome by good (Rom 12:21) KJV. You begin to love one another, care for one another and really respect people. My hunger and thirst for God was being satisfied. We must eat the Word of God each day.

# CHAPTER 4

# VEGETABLES AND FRUIT EXPERIENCE

Daniel and the Vegetarian Diet

Daniel 1:4, 5, 8, 12, 16, 17 (KJV)

... Children in whom no blemish, but well favored, and skillful in all wisdom, and cunning in knowledge, and understanding science, and such had ability in them to stand in the king's palace, and whom they might teach the learning and the tongue of Chaldeans.

... And the king appointed them a daily provision of the king's meat and the wine which he drank: nourishing them three years, that at the end thereof they might stand before the king. (Scofield, 898)

... Prove thy servants, I beseech thee, ten days; and let them give us pulse to eat, and water to drink.

... But Daniel purposed in his heart that he would not defile himself with the portion of the king's meat, nor with which he drank: therefore he requested of the prince of the eunuchs that he might not defile himself.

Daniel and the brethren

... Thus Melzer took away the portion of their meat, and the wine that they should drink; and gave them pulse (Lentils, chickpeas, legumes, vegetables).

... As for these four children God gave them knowledge and skill in all learning and wisdom: and Daniel had understanding in all vision and dreams. (Scofield, 899)

As we eat our fruit and vegetables we become wise.

What is wisdom? Well it's the quality of being wise, ability to make right use of knowledge and spiritual perception. Fruit and vegetables taste good and are good for you.

Gal. 5:22, 23(KJV)

... But the fruit of the Spirit is love, joy, peace, longsuffering, gentleness, goodness, faith.

... Meekness, temperance: against such there is no law (Scofield, 1247).

Daniel in his own right was a prophet. As an interpreter of visions and dreams, the tree vision was explained (Dan. 4:19-27), KJV. This righteous man prayed (Dan. 9:3-19), KJV. I find that we need fruit and vegetables for strength and nourishment.

Naturally, as a diabetic our physicians and nutritionist advise us to eat fruit and vegetables rather than to eat junk food. Spiritually you eat the right word, the Bible. Study the word and don't take in any junk. Examine your fruit and vegetables. Make sure that it is not rotten. Make sure that your prophet/shepherd is real and righteous. We are to train up a child in the way he should go: and when he is old, he will not depart from it (Prov. 22:6), KJV. The Lord uses children to minister to others. Our children need salvation in healing in their lives today.

# CHAPTER 5

# IT'S DINNER TIME

During our full course meal we have some meat. Meat is the flesh of animal used as food. The substance or essence eaten as food.

Heb. 5:14 (KJV)

But strong meat belongeth to them that are full of age, even those who by reason of use have their senses exercised to discern both good and evil (Scofield, 1295).

Lk. 5:1-5 (KJV)

… And it came to pass, that as the people pressed upon him to hear the Word of God, he stood by the lake of Gennesaret,

… And saw two ships standing by the lake: but the fishermen were gone out of them and were washing their nets.

… And he entered into one of the ships, which was Simon's and prayed him that he would thrust out a little from the land. And he sat down, and taught the people out of the ship.

… Now when he had left speaking, he said unto Simon, Launch out into the deep and let down your nets for a draught.

… And Simon answering said unto him, Master we have toiled all the night, and have taken nothing: nevertheless at thy word I will let down the net (Scofield, 1078).

If we are ready for our meat, we must follow the menu and eat the right meat. We obey God. Obedience is the state of being compliant with commands, instructions, dutiful submission to authority. Our meat must be well done.

A healthy diet keeps us alive and well. God loves us. The Word of God will keep us well balanced. Love beareth all things, endureth all things (1 Cor. 12:7), KJV. Love is a strong liking for someone or something. Love is long and kind. As we eat our meat faith, hope and love come. Love is the greatest (1 Cor. 13:4, 13) KJV. Our meat helps us to be ready for the rapture. The rapture is the state of being carried away with love, joy and extreme delight, to transport, ecstasy. When the Lord comes back for his people and the church, we will be caught up in the air (1 Cor. 15:51- 57), KJV.

No one knows when the rapture will exactly come, but we do know that time is winding up. We know that Jesus is coming back for His church without a spot or wrinkle. Are you ready? Have you been washed by the blood of Jesus Christ? Are you Saved, Sanctified and Filled with the Holy Ghost? Do you pray to God in your spiritual tongue? Are you working for Jesus? He's waiting and watching us all the time. Are you prepared for this event? Enjoy the Holy Ghost. Know that the end draweth nigh.

After the rapture comes the Tribulation.

Know that during the tribulation there will be even more mysterious world crisis, confusion and panic.

The Anti-Christ will rise up. If you look at the scriptures in Revelation 19:11; 20:12-15 KJV, you can relate to the coming events for yourself. This world must be ready for Jesus Christ or they will meet Satan. Are you ready? As you enjoy your dinner, eat all of your meat.

As I continue to enjoy my dinner I think about "God's Blessings".

Belief in His powers.

Love for your fellowman.

Established in the Word of God.

Saved and alive.

Sanctified and clean.

Inheritance of wisdom and knowledge.

New creature in Christ.

Grateful and filled with the Holy Ghost.

Satisfied in Jesus alone.

By Candace Strand

# CHAPTER 6

# DESSERTS-SWEET AND SOUR

Sometimes we can have some dessert. John the Baptist (end of an era), Jesus Christ (beginning of a new era). John the Baptist brought Jesus Christ for dessert.

(See Matt. 11:1-12) KJV

John the Baptist proclaimed: that the kingdom of heaven is at hand. Jesus Christ and John the Baptist were great, moral men born of humble women and cousins. Jesus Christ is free from and free for us. We are his disciples and he wants our souls. The holy Ghost is the evidence of this today. Our dessert is the Holy Ghost with power. The power boost or sugar rush is delicious. The anointing is real and we must take it by force! The anointing breaks yokes. It stops generational curses. Enjoy your sweet dessert.

Jer. 5:5 KJV says, I will get unto the great men and will speak unto them: for they have known the way of the Lord, and the judgement of their God; but these have altogether broken the yoke and burst the bonds. (Dake, 750).

Isa. 9:4 KJV says, For thou has broken the yoke of his burden, and the staff of his shoulder, the rod of his oppressor, as in the day of Midian (Dake, 687).

The sour desserts we throw away. There is no power, no strength, no nourishment. You can gain unnecessary weight. The yoke can be heavy, like in 1 Ki. 12 KJV and II Chron. 10:1-11 KJV. The people were rebellious against Rehoboam, also see 1 Ki. 12: 4, 9-11 KJV. The yoke of bondage is real. The ordeal/dessert was sour.

When we think about how rough it was back then, we should be glad that those iron yokes are not used today on us. Prisoners are bound by hand cuffs, that is a sour dessert. And you may think that a yoke is on you, but if you're filled with the Holy Ghost there should be no yoke on you. Your dessert will be tasty and good ... Yummy!

It was sweet when Jesus Christ came. It was sour when he was crucified on the cross. It was sweet when John the Baptist proclaimed about Jesus. It was sour when he was beheaded. As a Christian, sometimes we have some sour dessert but we have to learn to get the sweet dessert and enjoy it. We are Ambassadors for Christ (II. Cor. 5:20 KJV).

Strongholds are sour. We must pull down the strongholds. A stronghold is a place where doctrine is strongly upheld. (Geddes & Grosset, 375) Spiritual warfare is not sweet. We must know how to war in the spirit, as we deal with negative spiritual war against God (Berube, 916). We are the Lord's warriors with the fruit of the spirit. Are you a soldier in God's army? You have to put on all your armor for God. Our dessert becomes rich.

# CHAPTER 7

# SHREDDING WEIGHT

Shred – To cut or tear. Long irregular strip cut or torn off, particle, a small amount.

Weight – is the heaviness of a thing, consider, importance.

In shredding weight we must deal with Lucifer (Isa. 14:12 KJV), Satan (Zech. 3:1 KJV) and the Devil (Rev. 12:9 KJV), or whatever you want to call the enemy. We do not want any weight weighing us down. We must bind up that false spirit. We must:

| | |
|---|---|
| Trust God | Phil. 3:1-9 KJV |
| Confide in God | Titus 3:5 KJV (Strong, 235) |
| Submit to God/Jesus | I. Jn. 4:4 KJV |
| Don't give in to Satan | I. Pet. 5:8, 9 KJV (Strong, 228) |
| Watch out for wicked devices | II. Cor. 2:11 KJV |
| Be a well-equipped soldier | Eph. 6:11-18 KJV |

And cloth yourself with God's

Clothes.

We must shred (II. Tim 3:1-7 KJV)-The perils of a man of God. (Dake, 239) Lascivious(ness)-Voluntary sexual intercourse between a married person and partner other than the lawful spouse. Idolatry-Worship of idols, excessive devotion. Variance-Variation, difference of opinion, dispute, act contrary to usual rule.Wrath-Furious, often vindictive anger; rage, punishment or vengeance as a manifestation of anger. Strife-Heated, often volent dissension; bitter conflict; A struggle fight or quarrel. Sedition-Conduct or language inciting rebellion against the state; Insurrection, rebellion. Heresies-An opinion or doctrine at variance with religious orthodoxy. A controversial or unorthodox opinion or doctrine as politics, philosophy or science. (Dake, 239). Revelling-To take great pleasure or delight. To engage boisterous festivities. Witchcraft-Magic, sorcery Fornication-Sexual intercourse between partner who are not married; single. Uncleaness-Morally defiled, unchaste. Ceremonially impure. Foul or dirty. Hatred-Intense animosity or hostility. Murder-The unlawful killings of human by another esp. with premeditated malice.

We must also bind up the LGBTQ spirit, (Lev. 20:13), KJV. Homosexuality and Incest are sin. These sins and weights have to be shredded. (See Leviticus Chapters 18-20), KJV. These abominations do not please God!

As people shred weights of Satan, they will no longer be tempted, be an accuser, lie and be a deceiver. As we obey God no other spirits should be working in us. We are reconciled to God. We have reconciliation with God. We must re-establish a close relationship between ourselves and God. We must settle or resolve and bring (oneself to accept God's spirit). We must be compatible and consistent. In II. Cor. 5:19 KJV, it notes in this context Paul affirmed that God was Christ, reconciling the world unto himself. After weight is shred you will look Holy. You will be righteous. You will be pure and live right for the Lord. Oh, to be like Jesus ...

# CHAPTER 8

# DIMENSIONAL GROWTH

Dimension means width, length, height. A measure of spatial extent; scope, magnitude. (Berube, 243) Growth is the process of growing or developing. (Berube, 376) Growth is angel of light. Today it is the light of the world.

Can you say ... Shekinah Glory? Is there a presence of God in your life? Does God dwell in you?

Are the angels watching over you?

What are angels?

Greek word – Angelos (angeloi-plural)

Hebrew word – malak

It means messenger.

Under the Mosiac law (background) Exodus 25:17-25 KJV, (See Exod. 1:5-14; 28:12, 13,17) KJV, Some angels were good like Cheribims, Seraphim's, Gabriel, Michael and more. Also know that Satan is a fallen angel. There are plenty of them too like, (Belial and Beelzebub). So beware! Use your discernment.

Check out the mercy seat, and Ark of the Covenant and compare it to today.

We must pray, and strive for heaven. In heaven we have:

Outer

Inner

3rd realm – 3rd Heaven (See II. Cor 12:2 KJV)

(See I. Jn. 1:5-7 KJV / II. Cor. 11:13-15 KJV) (Rev. 1:11, 20 KJV)

Revelation of John: Messenger of the Seven churches. Seven Angels of the seven trumpets. Seven Angels of seven plagues. Four Angels of the four winds. Twenty-four elders in Heaven.

Know that: (Col. 1:16) KJV, God created the Angels

There are good and evil (fallen) angels

Beware of Demons (Matt. 24:41), KJV

They are unclean and familiar spirits like Jezebel, Delilah and Apollyon. "The Devil's Angels." Satan is a created angel and the author of sin. 1 I Jn. 4:4 KJV says, Ye are of God, little children, and have overcome them; because greater is he that is in you, then he that is in the world.

Dimensional brings about some miracles. It's a marvel. It's supernatural in origin. It is an act God. Only believe because the miracle is yours. Miracles are real.

Angels are spirit-servants.

The Lord can have angels do some things.

Rev. 16:1 KJV says, and I heard a great voice out of the temple saying to seven angels, Go your ways, and pour out the vial of wrath of God upon the earth.

Heb. 1:14 KJV says, are they not all ministering spirits, sent forth to minister for them who shall be heirs of salvation. (Scofield, 1292)

Revelation is inevitable. The word must come forth for all to hear. As we focus on God and bask in dimensional growth and the help of God we will reach higher heights and deeper depths in Christ. Heb. 11:16 KJV says, But now they desire a better country, that is, an heavenly: wherefore God is not be ashamed to, be called their God; for he hath prepared for them a city. We shall see God and be with the Lord someday.

---

1.  MacArthur, John. The MacArthur Bible Commentary. xviii.

# PART
# TWO

# SEEKING JESUS

Study to show yourself approved.
Enjoy the Word of God.
Enlighten others about God's goodness.
Kindness and grace towards all.

Joy, joy, joy
Everlasting life God's peace.
Salvation is free.
Universal happiness with God.
Strong, solid and sealed with the Holy Ghost.
By Candace Strand

# CHAPTER 9

# OBEDIENCE TO GOD

How do I obey God?

A.) Through Prayer

Acts 6:4 KJV says, But we will give ourselves continually to prayer, and to the ministry of the word. (Scofield, 1156)

We know that Adam was disobedient to God, but Jesus was obedient and now we have eternal life. The prayers of the righteous availeth much. The righteous shall see God. The Bible doesn't lie. Rom. 5:19 KJV says, For as by one man's disobedience many made sinners so by the obedience of one shall many be made righteous. (Scofield, 1198)

We must listen, follow and obey God. Obedience consists of; when, where and how we survive and act in this life. In being obedient you are called of God. It is a blessing to be called by God. For many are called, but few are chosen (Matt. 22:14), KJV (Scofield, 1030). When we pray, we must pray without ceasing. (I Thes. 5:17) KJV.

In order to get closer to the Lord we have to talk to God. Tell God everything so that our footsteps can be ordered of the Lord. Our obedience to God is an essential part to our supplications to him. We can petition God (Matt. 6:9-13), KJV.

### B.) Supplications and Fastings

Dan. 9:3 KJV says, And I set my face unto the Lord God, to seek by prayer and supplications with fastings and sackcloth and ashes. (Scofield, 913)

We must humbly ask the Lord to answer our prayers and to help us to obey God and the laws of the land. Obedience to God brings about a change in your life. Rebellion brings about error and confusion. When we turn down our plates and pray, the Holy Ghost begins to move. Prayers are answered. Things begin to happen. As we go through spiritual warfare we come out victorious. Adversity is bound up. Satan is defeated. We are thankful and grateful. We want to bless the Lord. Our hearts are full of thanksgiving.

When we fast we should be healthy. Try to keep a proper diet. Do not overexert ourself. Start out with a short one. Maybe 36 hours, once or twice a week. Eat fruit in the morning. You can work your way up to 3 day fast. You can drink fresh unsugar lemonade or light lemonade with a little honey or brown sugar or a little fruit juice. If you can rest and have an enema. To regain strength you can eat brown or white toasted bread, bananas, nuts, figs, berries, apples and vegetables. Fasting and prayer is wonderful. The Lord's Prayer: Matt. 6:9-13 (Message/Remix)

Our Father in heaven

Reveal who you are

Set the world right;

Do what's best—

As above, so below

Keep us alive with three square meals.

Keep us forgiven with you and forgiving others

Keep us safe from ourselves and the devil.

You're in charge!

You can do anything you want!

You're ablaze in beauty!

Yes. Yes. Yes. Message/Remix) (Peterson, 1437)

---

2.   Ehret, Arnold, Rational Fastings, 83.

# CHAPTER 10

# HUMBLE IS THE WAY

Humble is meek or modest, low in rank, lesser. (Berube, 415) Holiness is the way. You must repent, be baptized, In Jesus name and receive the Holy Ghost. (See Acts 2:38 KJV). If you live Holy you will be humble. Jesus is the answer. Jesus will keep you humble. When you are humble you are justified. (See Rom. 8:30, 33 KJV and Rom. 3:23-25 KJV).

Justification is a fact or circumstance that justifies. It helps you to demonstrate how to be just or valid. (Berube, 464). We are justified through faith. There are seven results of justification in Romans 5:1-11 (KJV). You have peace with God when you are humble and justified. Justified is derived from the Greek verb (dikaioo), which means "to acquit" or to declare righteous. It is also a term used in trials. When you realize this you are to still remain humble.

When you are humble you become righteous. Righteousness is morally upright, and just. II Cor. 5:21 KJV says, For he hath made him to be sin for us, who knew no sin: that we might be made the righteousness of God in him. (Dake, 195) Psm. 9:8 KJV says, And he shall judge the world in righteousness, he shall minister judgement to the people in uprightness. (Dake, 551) I Pet. 2:24 KJV says, who his own self bare our sins in his own body on the tree, that we, being dead to sins, should live unto righteousness: by whose stripes ye were healed. (Dake, 266)

When you are in holiness you become humble.

Holiness

(See I Pet. 1:14-16 KJV Heb. 12:14 KJV ; Isa. 35:8 KJV; Lev. 11:44 KJV)

Holiness is used in many ways:

1. Of God's true nature – Psm. 30:4 KJV; Psm. 97:12KJV
2. In signets on the high priest's mitre – Psm. 28:36 KJV; Psm. 39:30 KJV
3. Of worship to God – I Chr. 16:29 KJV; Psm. 29:2 KJV; Psm. 96:9 KJV
4. Of praise to God – II Chr. 20:21 KJV
5. To God - II Chr. 31:18 KJV
6. Of God's throne – Psm. 47:8 KJV
7. Of God's dwelling – Psm. 48:1 KJV; Isa. 63:15 KJV; Jer. 23:9 KJV; Jer. 31:23 KJV
8. Of God's revelation – Psm. 60:6 KJV; Psm. 108 KJV
9. Of God's oath – Psm. 89:35 KJV; Amos 4:2 KJV
10. Of God's house – Psm. 93:5 KJV ; Isa. 62:9 KJV
11. Of consecrated things – Isa. 23:18 KJV
12. Of a literal highway leading up to the temple of God – Isa. 35:8 KJV
13. Of God's people – Isa. 63:18 KJV

14. Of human society – Oba. 17 KJV
15. Inscriptions on bells and pots
16. Of God's spirit – Rom. 1:4 KJV
17. Of Christian living – Rom. 6:19, 22 KJV; II Cor. 7:1 KJV; I Tim. 2:15 KJV; Titus 2:3 KJV; Heb. 12:10, 14 KJV
18. Of the eternal state and nature of believers in heaven – I Thes. 3:13 KJV (Dake, 110)

As we continue to be humble and live holy we should count our blessings.

# WORDS OF ENCOURAGEMENT

Christ delivers.
Observe good works.
Understand the truth.
Neither is there salvation in any other.
Trust in the Lord and do good.

Yearn for Jesus.
Obey God's Word.
Use your mind.
Remember Jesus always.

Build a strong foundation.
Learn of God's ways.
Evaluate your soul salvation.
Sin no mor.
Serve Jesus.
Investigate, grow, and gain God's power.
Nurture Christ's power.
Give with love.
Spiritually grow and mature in Christ.

COUNT YOUR BLESSINGS- BY Candace Strand

# CHAPTER 11

# COMPASSION BUILDS CHARACTER

You must be compassionate toward others. Jesus was compassionate. He shed his blood for us. We are redeemed by the blood of the lamb. The cross and Jesus's name represent the blood. (Heb. 9:22) KJV.

Almost all things are by the law purged with blood; and without shedding of blood is no remission. Character steps

1. Reconciliation. We are reconciled through Christ. (Rom. 5:8-10) KJV; 8. But God commendeth His love towards us, in that, while we were yet sinners, Christ died for us. 9. Much more then, being now justified by his blood, we shall be saved from wrath through him. (Scofield, 1197) 10. For if, when we were enemies, we reconciled to God by the death of his Son, much more, being reconciled, we shall be saved by his life. (Butler, 1168)
2. Reconciliation term is found in Paul's epistles.

3. Sanctification. Set aside for the service of God. It's not in the clothes. Make sure that you are sanctified. Sanctification can also mean to sanctify, to consecrate and purify. It comes from the Latin word santificatio, meaning the act/process of making holy, consecrated. In Greek it looks like this: (Hag, hagiasmos, hagasyne and hagotes-(holiness). II Cor. 6:17 KJV says, Wherefore come out from among them, and be ye separate, saith the Lord, and touch not the unclean thing; and I will receive you (Butler, 1230). I Thes. 5:22, 23 KJV says, Abstain from all appearance of evil. And the very God of peace sanctify you wholly; and I pray God your whole spirit and soul and body be preserved blameless unto the coming of our Lord Jesus Christ (Scofield, 1270).

God is not slack. II Pet. 3:9 KJV says, The Lord is not slack concerning his promise, as some men count slackness; but is longsuffering to-us-ward, not willing that they should perish, but that all should come to repentance (Scofield, 1319). The Lord is compassionate towards people.

Compassion of Jesus

What is going on?

There is : The Mosaic covenant, the law and commandments, Deut. 5 KJV (read and learn about it). The Jew and Gentile yesterday and today. (The Hebrew and the Greek). Eph 2:4-18 KJV says, Jew and Gentile one body in Christ; For he is our peace, who hath made both one, and hath broken down the middle wall of partition between us; Having abolished in his flesh the enmity, even the law of commandments contained in ordinances; for to make in himself of twain one new man, so making peace; And that he might reconcile both God in one body by the cross, having slain the enmity thereby;

And came and preached peace to you which were afar, off, and to them were nigh. For through him we both have access by one Spirit unto the Father. (Scofield, 1251)

As you can see the word of God helped me to understand the compassion of Jesus. Rom. 1:16 KJV says, For I am not ashamed of the gospel of Christ. For it is the power of God unto salvation to everyone that believeth, to the Jew first and also to the Greek (Scofield, 1192). Gal. 3:28 KJV there is neither Jew nor Greek, there is neither bond nor free, male nor female: for ye are all one in Christ Jesus. (Scofield, 1245)

Today, we have (Mark 13:7, 8 KJV); Matt. 24:4-14) KJV :

War and rumors of war

Famine in the land

Earthquakes, tornadoes, hurricane, storms

Disease

Greed, prosperity issues

Etc.

New Covenant

Today there is grace and mercy, but how long is it going to last? Don't wait until it is too late to build your compassion that God wants you to have. With God's compassion, Jesus shed his blood, sacrificed, share and gave to us. Make the new covenant with God. The blood makes the difference. As you obey God and the covenant your destiny is near. The word of God in Jer. 31:31-37 KJV says, that Behold, the days come, saith the Lord, that I will make a new covenant with the house of Israel, and with the house of Judah; Not according to the covenant that I made with their fathers in the day that I took them by the hand to bring them out of the land of Egypt: which my covenant the brake, although I was an husband unto them, saith the Lord, I will put my law in their inward parts, and write it in their hearts; and will be their God, and they shall be my people. And they shall teach no more every man is neighbor, and every man his brother, saying, Know the Lord: for they shall all know me, from the least of them unto the greatest of them, saith the Lord; for I will forgive their iniquity, and I will remember their sins no more. Thus saith the Lord, which giveth the sun for a light by light by day, and the ordinances of the moon and of the stars for a light by night, which divideth the sea when the waves thereof roar; The Lord of host is his name; If those ordinances depart from before me saith the Lord, then the seed of Israel also shall cease from being a nation before me forever. Thus saith the Lord; If heaven above can be measured, and the foundations of the earth searched out beneath, I will also cast off all the seed of Israel for all that they have done, saith the Lord (Scofield, 806).

# CHAPTER 12

# SACRIFICE AND LEARN RESPECT

Offer unto the Lord. Bring your offerings to God. You may have to sacrifice. Know that the Lord will intervene. The Bible tells us to in Mal. 3:10 (Message/Remix) : Bring your full tithe to the temple treasury so there will be ample provision in my temple. Test me in this and see if I don't open up heaven itself to you and pour out blessings beyond your wildest dreams. (Peterson, 1421)

As you strive to reach your destiny you will sacrifice. You may have tithes or you may try to determine whether to pay tithes or pay your rent. What do you do? Respect the Lord and reverence God. God will open doors for you. The Lord will provide. There's a song that I like to sing. I will paraphrase it for you. The song says, that even if you can not see your way. If you are doing all that you can do. The Lord has not forgotten you. You must hold your head up. Be true to the Lord. The Lord will open doors for you. You fight for God through dark times. You might be heavy laden. You do not see any way. But know that God our Lord will open doors for us all.

List three ways that you have sacrificed for Jesus:

1.

2.

3.

As we sacrifice for Christ, the Lord will reward us openly.

We are told to:

Respect our elders and people.

Respect the and.

Respect God.

Spiritually, feel good. Your destiny towards God's kingdom is near. Offer yourself unto the Lord. Rom. 12:1 KJV says, that I, beseech you therefore, brethren, by the mercies of God, that ye present your bodies as a living sacrifice, holy, acceptable unto God, which is your reasonable service.

Write your thoughts about, "Respecting our Savior"

Where are you as far as reaching your destiny?

# CHAPTER 13

# HAPPINESS, PEACE, JOY IN THE HOLY GHOST

Happiness is glee in the Holy Ghost. I can fly like eagle in the spirit. I am happy in Jesus Christ. I sing because I am happy. I sing because I am free. My favorite song is "His eye is on the Sparrow" because I know that the Lord watches over me. I do not feel discouraged. I am happy because Jesus loves me and that feels good. I can say Amen.

The Lord will keep in perfect peace in the Holy Ghost. You have to keep your mind stayed on Jesus. Focus is the key to peace. God is not author of confusion. God will keep your inner man calm. We are to be content in every situation. Emotions are not a part of peace. We are alive in Christ and peacemakers. Blessed are the peacemakers: for they shall be called the children of God. (Matt. 5:9 KJV) (Scofield, 999) also see (Gal. 5:22 KJV).

Joy is praise in the Holy Ghost. I will praise the Lord according to his righteousness: and will sing praise to the name of the most high. (Psm. 7:17 KJV,) (Scofield, 602). I will be glad and rejoice in

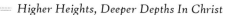 

thee; I will sing praise to thy name, O thou most High. (Psm. 9:2 KJV) (Scofield, 603). Great is the Lord, and greatly to be praised in the city of our God, in the mountain of His holiness (Psm. 48:1 KJV), (Scofield, 621). Restore unto me the joy of thy salvation, and uphold me with thy free spirit. (Psm. 51:12 KJV), (Scofield, 624). I will praise the name of God with a song, and will magnify him with thanksgiving. (Psm. 69:30 KJV), (Scofield, 632).

Oh people. We must magnify the Lord. We must exalt the Lord's name together!

Write about your happiness in the Holy Ghost.

Write about your peace in the Holy Ghost.

Write about your Joy in the Holy Ghost.

# CHAPTER 14

# RIGHTEOUS AND HOLY LIVING VS. SATAN AND SIN

There's a war going on. Are you well equipped? Do you have on the whole armour of God? Satan is always busy, seeking whom he may devour. We know that in Ephesians 6:11 KJV, it says to put on the whole armour of God, that ye may be able to stand against the wiles of the devil. We must gird up our loins, we need the breastplate of righteousness, our feet shod with the preparation of the gospel of peace, we need the shield of faith; the helmet of salvation and the sword of God, which is the Word of God.

As a Christian we must be strong in the Lord and in the power of his might. We must fast, pray and watch. Be on guard. Be alert and a willing worker for Jesus. Be a true warrior for the Lord. Let us beat the devil. Have faith in God.

Satan is a deceiver and a defeated foe. As a deceiver the devil brings about sin. We were born in sin and shaped in iniquity. Satan fooled Adam and Eve. (Gen. 31 KJV). Satan is subtil. Because of sin Cain killed Abel, his own brother. Because of sin the tower of Babel existed. Abomination is homosexuality a major sin of today. This deceiver is a liar.

A righteous man hateth lying: but a wicked man is loathsome and cometh to shame. (Prov. 13:5 KJV) The works of the flesh are adultery, fornication, uncleaness, lasciviousness, idoltry, witchcraft, hatred, variance, emulations, wrath, strife, seditions, heresies, envyings, murders, drunkenness, revellings, they which do such things shall not inherit the kingdom of God. (Scofield, 1247)

Rom. 6:23 KJV says, For the wages of sin is death; but the gift of God is eternal life through Jesus Christ. (Scofield, 1199)

Righteous and Holy living requirers you to Sanctify yourselves therefore, and be ye holy: for I am holy: for I am the Lord your God (Lev. 2:7 KJV).

We must live holy and live right and not be deceived by the devil and the world to commit sin. Ask for forgiveness and love Jesus. Eph. 6:20 KJV says, For which I am an ambassador in bond: that therein I may speak boldly, as I ought to speak (Scofield, 1255)

I had to learn how to live holy and to live right. You don't want to become self- righteous. This process will keep you humble and meek. Well, Jesus was humble and powerful. You love the Lord with your whole heart, soul and being. You bind up the devil. You must pray without ceasing. Pray in the spirit because the Lord will hear your petition unto him. Don't you just love God? You have to learn how to forgive also. God forgave us. He died on the cross for us and forgave us. There should be no excuse.

Find the Words:

But seek ye first the kingdom of God, and his righteousness; and all these things shall be added unto you. (Matt. 6:33) KJV

| | | | | | | | | | | | | | |
|---|---|---|---|---|---|---|---|---|---|---|---|---|---|
| B | U | T | O | R | S | V | D | L | R | X | K | L | M |
| Y | X | W | Y | I | T | U | F | M | S | Y | J | N | O |
| L | M | S | E | E | K | A | G | N | T | Z | I | P | Q |
| Z | D | A | B | L | E | T | H | O | U | Z | E | F | J |
| I | J | O | K | T | H | E | A | P | V | A | F | G | H |
| K | I | N | G | D | O | M | Q | W | B | C | D | E | O |
| D | A | O | F | S | G | O | D | U | N | T | O | Y | W |
| C | B | A | N | D | C | F | I | R | S | T | Z | X | U |
| H | I | S | D | A | T | R | S | W | A | L | L | S | C |
| A | R | I | G | H | T | E | O | U | S | N | E | S | S |
| B | D | J | K | L | M | H | E | F | I | D | T | U | Y |
| N | O | P | Q | R | B | E | W | S | R | V | W | X | I |
| A | D | D | E | D | E | S | H | A | L | L | Z | T | V |
| C | W | Y | O | U | T | E | T | H | I | N | G | S | I |

# CHAPTER 15

# HOW TO GIVE AND RECEIVE

Ae you a giver? You must:

1.  Give an offering to God. You will receive from the Lord. The Lord will prosper you. The Lord will take care of you. Just say Jesus, we need you … Jesus we love you …

    Tithes

    (Mal. 3:10) KJV

    Bring ye all the tithes into the storehouse, that there may be meat in mine house, and prove me now herewith, saith the Lord of hosts, if I will not open you the windows of heaven, and pour you out a blessing, that there shall not be room enough to receive it.

Name                    Benefit
Jehovah – Jireh         Success

Meaning – Jehovah's provision shall be seen. You are our provider. Your name is great.

2. Give your time to God. Pray and worship the Lord. Seek the Lord.
3. Give your soul to Jesus, knowing that it will be worth it all. You will receive God's marvelous works.
4. As you give and receive under the will of God, you will find the experience very gratifying and rewarding.

Food for thought:

Psm.37:11 KJV says, But the meek shall inherit the earth; and shall delight themselves in the abundance of peace (Scofield, 616).

Phil. 4:3 KJV says, And I intreat thee also, true yokefellow, help those women which labored with me in the gospel, Clement also, and with other fellow labourers, whose names are in the book of life. (Scofield, 1260)

As a minister of the gospel (MDIV-LTSP-2013), I count it an honor. Some people don't accept women Pastors, but the word of God says, that your sons and daughters shall prophesy (Acts 2:17 KJV), (Joel 2:28 KJV), (Jer. 3:15 KJV). I believe God and I am humbled, available and qualified "In Jesus name."

Neh. 8:10 KJV says, Then he saith unto them, Go your way, eat the fat, and drink the sweet and send portions unto them for whom nothing is prepared: for this day is holy unto our Lord: neither be ye sorry; for the joy of the Lord is your strength. (Scofield, 549)

III Jn. 2 (KJV) says, Beloved I wish above all things that thou mayest prosper and be in health, even as thy soul prospereth. (Scofield, 1327).

5. Receive the Word of God. Obey the Word of God. Live by the Word of God. Stand on the Word of God.

Food for thought

Sow and Reap benefits:

Gal. 6: 7, 8 (KJV) Be not deceived; God is not mocked: for whatsoever a man soweth, that shall he also reap. For he that soweth to his flesh shall of the flesh reap corruption; but he that soweth to the spirit shall of the spirit reap life everlasting. (Scofield, 1247) We want eternal life!.. ...

Luke 8:11 (KJV) Now the parable is this: The seed is the Word of God. (Scofield, 1083). We need the Word of God. We can minister the Word of God ... Amen!

II Cor. 9: 6,7 (KJV) But this I say, He which soweth sparingly shall reap sparingly; and he which soweth bountifully shall reap bountifully. Every man according as he purposeth in his heart, so let him give not grudging, or of necessity: for God loveth a cheerful giver. (Scofield, 1236)

II Jn. 3:22 (KJV) And whatsoever we ask, we receive of him, because we keep his commandments, and do those things that are pleasing in his sight. (Scofield, 1324)

God's got a blessing for you. It does not mean to play the lottery of numbers. But miracles can happen. See Matt. 17:24 (KJV).

Food for thought

Matt. 7:7 (KJV)
Ask, and it shall be given you: seek, and ye shall find: knock, and it shall be opened unto you.

| | | | | | | | | |
|---|---|---|---|---|---|---|---|---|
| C | D | A | O | P | E | N | E | D |
| A | N | D | V | S | H | A | L | L |
| C | S | P | L | I | T | J | K | S |
| M | L | K | T | S | A | N | D | H |
| N | Y | E | C | H | B | E | C | A |
| S | E | E | K | A | Y | O | U | L |
| Y | O | T | R | L | C | Y | E | L |
| N | L | S | T | L | D | U | V | W |
| G | I | V | E | N | F | I | N | D |
| C | P | K | N | O | C | K | L | M |
| R | S | T | Q | L | A | N | O | P |
| D | V | I | T | N | N | B | E | Q |
| U | N | T | O | Y | D | R | S | T |
| L | R | O | S | O | U | V | Y | Z |
| C | B | N | T | U | W | X | A | C |

# CHAPTER 16

# IT'S YOUR SEASON

As you become closer to completing the steps towards your destiny, speak those things as though they were. We must walk in it ... To everything there is a season, and a time to every purpose under heaven (Eccl. 3:1 KJV) (Dake, 669). Do not help God, but wait on him. The Lord will lead, guide and direct your footsteps.

Your destiny is one's inevitable fate. A predetermined course of events. It is power or agency thought to predetermine events. Live for your destiny. The Lord will reward you. After this manner thereforepray ye: Our Father which art in heaven, Hallowed be thy name. (Matt. 6:9 KJV), (Scofield, 1002). It's your season to walk in your calling. It is the will of God concerning you.

Will is the mental faculty by which one deliberately chooses a course of action. Self-discipline. A desire, purpose or determination. God said to stay in his will. For the weapons of our warfare are not carnal, but mighty through God to the pulling down of strongholds. (Dake, 197). Do not be carnal. The Lord will supply your every need (II Cor. 10:4 KJV). Each season takes us closer and loser to the End times. (Rev. 22:7 KJV) (Dake, 304). Behold, I come quickly: blessed is he that keepeth the sayings of the prophecy of this book. Do not give up and throw in the towel. Listen to the voice of God. Thy will be done. (Rev. 22:20 KJV). He which testifieth these things, saith Surely I come quickly. Amen. (Dake, 305). If you stay in God's will your goals will be achieved. Your prayers will be answered and God will open doors of your destiny. God will give you visions and dreams.

Visions are an unusual foresight. Amental image produced by the imagination. The experience of seeing the supernatural as if with the eyes. Acts 2:17, 18 (KJV) says, And it shall come to pass in the last days, saith God, I will por out my spirit upon all flesh and your sons and your daughters shall prophesy, and your young men shall see visions and your old men shall dream dreams. And on my servants and on my handmaidens I will pour out in those days of my Spirit; and they shall prosper . (Dake, 123)

Strive to reach your destiny with God.

Know that:

It's a new season, it's a new day. It's a season of power coming your way. During the season of power and prosperity, there's a great anointing coming your way. You have to know when it is your season. Walk with it. God will take care of you.

# FOOTNOTES

1  Macarthur, John. The MacArthur Bible Commentary. xviii.
2  Ehret, Arnold. Rational Fastings. 83.

## ANNOTATED BIBLIOGRAPHY

Berube, Margery s. The American Heritage Dictionary. Houghton Mifflin Company, 2001.

Butler, Trent. Holmon Bible Dictionary. Holmon Bible Publishers. 1991.

Dake, Finis Jennings. Dake's Annotated reference KJV Bible, Lawrenceville, Georgia, Printed in the USA, 1963, 1991.

Ehret, Arnold. Rational Fastings. Benedict Lust Publications, 1971.

Geddes & Grosset. Webster's Dictionary and Thesaurus with Color Atlas. Geddes & Grosset. 2002.

Mac Arthur, John. The Mac Arthur Bible Commentary. Nashville, Tennessee, by Thomas Nelson. 2005.

Peterson, Eugene H. The Message/Remix (The Bible in Contemporary Language), Colorado Springs, Co. Navpress, 2003, 2006.

Scofield, C.I. The Old Scofield Study KJV Bible (Standard Edition). Oxford University Press. 1917.

Strong, James. The New Strong's exhaustive Concordance of the Bible. Thomas Nelson Publishers. 1981.

This book has taken some time to complete. I thank God for the encouragement. Living Holy was not always a way for me. Growing up in a denominational church was all that I knew but God had another plan for me. I had to live the book. Growing higher and deeper in the Lord is a daily walk. You start as a baby, then adolescence, then you're an adult. You also may hit some bumps in the road but you eventually get there, to your destination. Prayer is important and faith unlocks the door. Without prayer and guidance from the Lord you will be walking in your flesh to fulfill your destiny walk and challenge. You set goals but the Lord may have other plans for you. If you are obedient to the spirit of God you will begin a different journey then you thought you originally thought you would have followed. The word is powerful and sharper than any two-edged sword. Follow it. The road may not be easy, but just sit back and enjoy the ride with Jesus. Use this book as your guide during your spiritual walk with the Lord. The trip is worth it. (Heb. 4:12 KJV) Continue to press toward the mark and you'll get there. Hold on to God's unchanging hand. (Phil. 3:14 KJV) For truly we can depend on God.

*Candace L. Strand MDIV (LTSP)*
BS Urban Ministry Leadership (CUTS)
BA Elementary Education

Printed in the United States
by Baker & Taylor Publisher Services